THE
Archive Photographs
SERIES

THE
GREAT EASTERN
RAILWAY

The scene at the well known gateposts and incline which led up from Liverpool Street Station's West Side suburban services. A drift of passengers suggests this is a mid-morning view around 1908. Note the shed-like structure inside the gates on the right which may be a police box.

THE
Archive Photographs
SERIES

THE
GREAT EASTERN
RAILWAY

Compiled by
Gavin Smith

CHALFORD

First published 1996
Copyright © Gavin Smith, 1996

The Chalford Publishing Company
St Mary's Mill, Chalford,
Stroud, Gloucestershire, GL6 8NX

ISBN 0 7524 0639 6

Typesetting and origination by
The Chalford Publishing Company
Printed in Great Britain by
Redwood Books, Trowbridge

Dedicated to Peter Ward, life-long railway man

Railway lines either side of St Mary's church and vicarage, Silvertown. Gaps in the fence allow pedestrians to cross the track on the left. Goods wagons await unloading with tarpaulin covers removed. A crowd of onlookers in the middle roadway watch the cameraman at work, c. 1904.

Contents

The Great Eastern Railway (G.E.R.) emblem as seen extensively on railway carriages, notices, publicity and in multiple other uses. Designed by Henry Parker, at Stratford Works, it incorporated coats of arms of counties such as Essex and Hetfordshire and towns and cities through which the G.E.R. passed. Pride of place in the centre were those of the City of London.

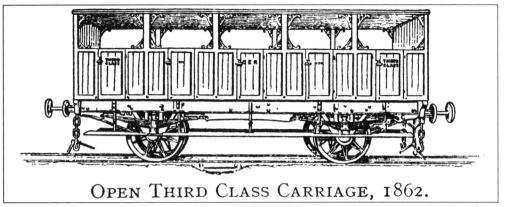

OPEN THIRD CLASS CARRIAGE, 1862.

Open third class carriage of 1862. Not a very comfortable ride, without the benefit of windows and smooth riding bogies and with hard seats, the early passenger was jolted all the way to his destination.

Introduction

This book is intended to be a celebration of the personality of the Great Eastern Railway up to its merger and grouping in 1923. Some may think that a railway company could not possibly have such a thing as a personality. If they believe this then they have never studied the romantic rise of the great nineteenth century companies. It is true that few are alive who know from personal experience the corporate loyalty that passengers and staff showed to their local lines before 1923. On the other side of London and the Country, the Great Western retained its name and identity after the grouping and went on to become a legend in the public arena. This lionisation reached tremendous heights and the line gained the popular appellation of 'God's Wonderful Railway' The Great Eastern with less glamourous material to work with should, I maintain, be henceforth known as 'Gods Excellent Railway', for its efficiency, organisation and the incredible number of passengers who passed through Liverpool Street daily, taking a Great Eastern train. The Great Eastern was a true pioneer, serving a large constituency (a whole swathe of England to the East and North of London, an area teeming with commuters plus the great spaces of East Anglia to the seacoast beyond). It even made a play for through traffic to Yorkshire and the North. The technical staff of the line were responsible for all kinds of innovations such as an early version of the electric signal box. Development of railtrack technology, and the operation of an intensive suburban steam service that amazed its rivals and challenged the reputed superiority of electric traction for suburban capacity.

The Great Eastern's successes grew out of the struggles of the earlier years. Its predecessors such as the Eastern Counties which operated the main line to Colchester (it had originally hoped to reach Ipswich and Yarmouth), the Eastern Union which took over the route to Ipswich and Norwich, and the Northern and Eastern running from a junction with the Eastern Counties at Stratford to Bishops Stortford all fought against great financial difficulties. Traffic in East Anglia was sparse and capital to extend and connect up with other routes was therefore hard to come by. Even after the formation of the Great Eastern in 1862, amalgamating all of the smaller lines mentioned, the outlook remained gloomy and at one point in 1867 it was in chancery, a Receiver was controlling receipts and payments and many of the locomotives of the company bore metal plates of creditors who rented them back to the G.E.R..

In the nick of time, the directors convened a meeting of the whole of the preference shareholders at which it was decided to apply to Parliament for authority to raise £3 million of debenture stock, giving the shareholders to great deal of control over the future. Fortunately this Bill was passed by Parliament and led to a new atmosphere of optimism which carried the company to new success. In 1874 the first part of the new Liverpool Street Station was opened – the old Bishopsgate terminus had been inconveniently placed for the City and the new one was to grow and grow again, ending up twice as big as the original building on the site. The magnificent hotel here with its accommodation, dining and meeting rooms put the Great Eastern on the map. A newly appointed Chairman leading the company on to great things was Lord Cranborne, soon to succeed to the title of the Marquis of Salisbury and eventually to become Prime Minister of Great Britain and Ireland. By 1900 the Chairmanship was in the hands of another able Chairman, Lord Claude Hamilton after whom a famous class of engines was to be named, familiar to every boy in love with railways.

This portrayal of the spirit of the Great Eastern can not possibly provide technical information about the railway – for this one looks to a lasting legacy of the line's lure – the Great Eastern Railway Society and its North Woolwich Station Museum. Members of the Society can provide information on nearly every corner of the G.E.R.'s activities of which we can only glimpse a small part. In closing it should be mentioned that pressure from such enthusiasts as these has led to the reconstruction of much of the glorious steel and glass roofscape of Liverpool Street Station in a tremendously effective way, so that what could have been a disastrous modernisation of the station, swamped in concrete, has become a superb memorial of a brilliant historic enterprise. Long live the Great Eastern Railway and all its works!

Arrival of Queen Victoria at Tottenham Station (Eastern Counties Railway) in 1847 with a pavilion built especially for her visit. Surprisingly enthusiastic about railway travel, she was en route to Cambridge.

One
Early Tracks

In this 1930s air view Bishopsgate Goods Station sprawls across the centre surrounded by a network of important roads. Not quite close enough to the City, this was G.E.Rs early terminus inherited from the Eastern Counties.

The impressive frontage of the enlarged Bishopsgate Terminus of the Eastern Counties Railway, originally known as 'Shoreditch'. Additions to the train accommodation were made several times after its opening on 1 July, 1840.

The arrival of the Christmas trains inside Bishopsgate Terminus, 1850. Although one separate luggage van can be seen, much of the luggage has been carried on the roof of the carriages.

13

THE EASTERN COUNTIES' RAILWAY
IS NOW OPEN

FROM THE TEMPORARY STATION, DEVONSHIRE STREET, NEAR MILE END TURNPIKE, TO

ROMFORD.

PASSENGER TRAINS WILL START AS FOLLOWS:

FROM LONDON.

MORNING.
15 minutes to 10 o'Clock.
*15 minutes past 11 „

AFTERNOON.
15 minutes to 2 o'Clock.
15 minutes past 3 „
15 minutes to 5 „
15 minutes past 6 „
15 minutes to 8 „

FROM ROMFORD.

MORNING.
9 o'Clock.
30 minutes past 10 „
*12 „

AFTERNOON.
30 minutes past 2 o'Clock.
4 „
30 minutes past 5 „
7 „

LEAVING THE INTERMEDIATE STATIONS, VIZ.:—

STRATFORD.

DOWN TRAINS.
MORNING. ABOUT
5 minutes to 10
*25 minutes past 11
AFTERNOON.
5 minutes to 2
25 minutes past 3
5 minutes to 5
25 minutes past 6
5 minutes to 8

UP TRAINS.
MORNING. ABOUT
23 minutes past 9
7 minutes to 11
3 minutes past 12
AFTERNOON.
7 minutes to 3
23 minutes past 4
7 minutes to 6
23 minutes past 7

ILFORD.

DOWN TRAINS.
MORNING. ABOUT
4 minutes past 10
*26 minutes to 12
AFTERNOON.
4 minutes past 2
26 minutes to 4
4 minutes past 5
26 minutes to 7
4 minutes past 8

UP TRAINS.
MORNING. ABOUT
14 minutes past 9
16 minutes to 11
*14 minutes past 12
AFTERNOON.
16 minutes to 3
14 minutes past 4
16 minutes to 6
14 minutes past 7

THE TRAINS WILL NOT RUN ON SUNDAY AT THE HOURS MARKED *

TABLE OF FARES.

	STRATFORD			ILFORD			ROMFORD		
	1st Class.	2nd Class.	3rd Class.	1st Class.	2nd Class.	3rd Class.	1st Class.	2nd Class.	3rd Class.
ROMFORD.							1s. 6d.	1s.	9d.
ILFORD.				1s.	9d.	6d.	2s.	1s. 6d.	1s.
STRATFORD.				1s. 6d.	1s.	9d.	2s. 6d.	1s. 6d.	1s.
LONDON.	9d.	6d.	4d.	1s. 6d.	1s.	9d.	2s. 6d.	1s. 6d.	1s.

Passengers and Parcels may be Booked at all the above-named Stations, at

**THE GLOUCESTER COFFEE-HOUSE, PICCADILLY;
BULL AND MOUTH, REGENT CIRCUS;
MOORE'S, OLD GREEN MAN AND STILL, 122, OXFORD STREET;
AND THE THREE NUNS, ALDGATE.**

Omnibuses conveying Passengers and Parcels to and from the Trains, call regularly at the above Offices, and Romford Coaches (in connexion with the Railway,) run daily to and from Brentwood, Chelmsford, Hornchurch, Upminster, and Ockenden.

The Servants of the Company are strictly prohibited from receiving any Fee or Gratuity whatever.

ADELAIDE PLACE, LONDON BRIDGE,
August, 1839.

Views of the early stations were commissioned as the public gradually become attuned to this dramatic new form of travelling. Elsenham Station seems to consist principally of the Stationmaster's house. The compact early engines were bought in from a number of manufacturers before the companies began to set up their own erecting shops.

Right: The unusual Chesterford Station, built in 1845 (architect Francis Thompson) had a symmetrical design and excellent platform canopy to protect waiting passengers. What remains of this design is now a Grade II listed building.

Opposite: The first timetable of 1839, which mentions the system of connecting road vehicles and London booking offices in the West End. The rail connection to the London Terminus and the line beyond Romford were yet to be completed.

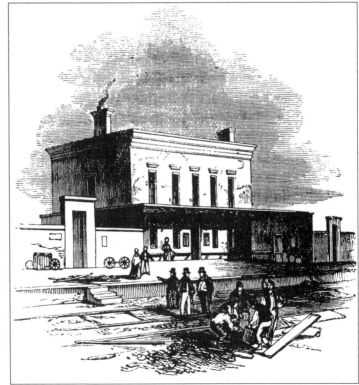

SIDE VIEW OF IM

The beginning of the long process of improvement in passenger carriage design. These sketches from 1847 show designs for new rolling stock for the North Woolwich branch of the Eastern Counties Railway, manufactured at Adams Fairfield Works, Bow. The Dimensions, 40 feet in

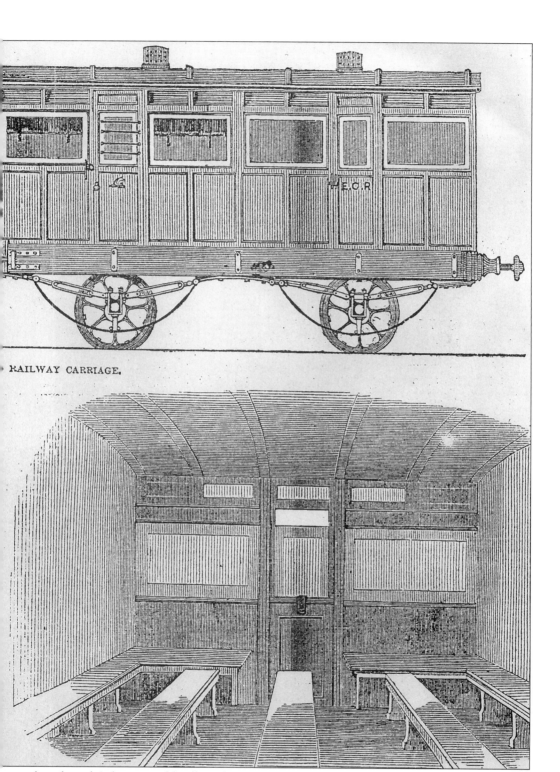

RAILWAY CARRIAGE.

length and 9 feet in width allowed a passage through the whole of the interior which was unusual at the time and for many years to come.

Brandon Station – note the railway policeman directing the trains. These officers also acted as signalmen. In 1845 two new railways joined at Brandon to complete a route to Norwich via Cambridge from London, instead of the originally planned route via Colchester.

This solid metal drinking fountain was built into the wall of the goods shed next to the down platform of Tottenham Station. Bearing the date 1860 and the head of Queen Victoria it expresses the pride and optimism of the new railway age.

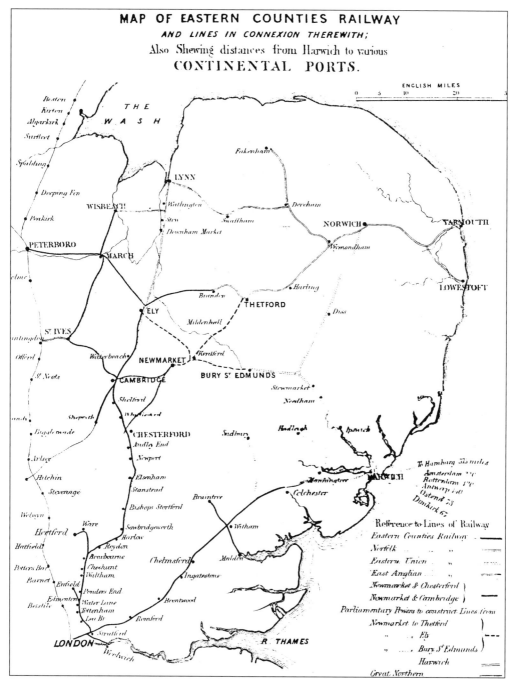

Eastern Counties system map showing the Northern and Eastern Railway from Stratford to Newport now incorporated in the Eastern Counties. The Norfolk Railway runs south from Norwich to Brandon to link up with the Eastern Counties extension from Newport via Cambridge and Ely to Brandon.

Stratford Works, 1851. The first Eastern Counties Railway factory was at Romford, a building which still exists beside the railway at Squirrel's Heath. In 1848 development began at the new works at Stratford to which activities were transferred. The Northern and Eastern Railway

Stratford Junction, 1851. The two stations on either side of the junction can be clearly seen. The Northern and Eastern Railway ran to the left. Its route aiming for Cambridge received

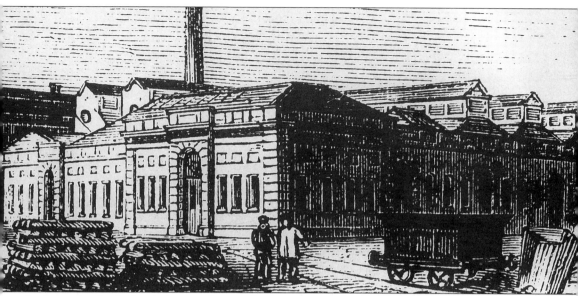

had previously built their roundhouse for locomotives here which can be seen in the background of this view.

approval on the same day as the Eastern Counties to Colchester, Ipswich and Norwich, on the right.

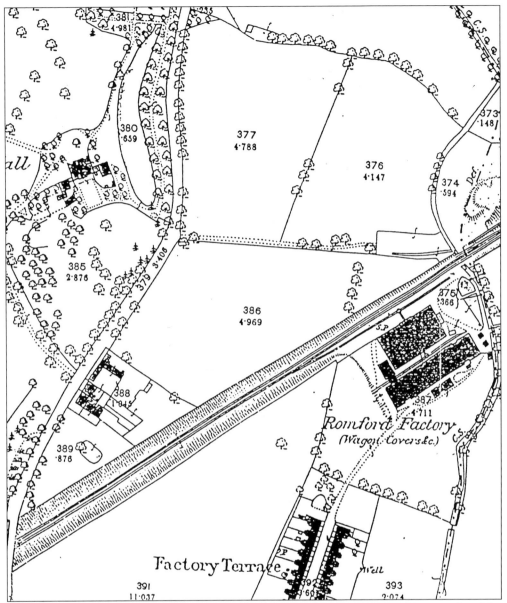

Map showing the Squirrels Heath Factory, c. 1870. This had been the original loco works of the E.C.R. for a few years but by this date had become a manufactory for wagon covers and a store. Factory Terrace housed Great Eastern workers and their families nearby.

An air-view in the late 1920s showing the original Squirrels Heath Works from the south. The compact 1843 buildings are identified by their round-headed windows while later additions had square windows. A brand new store stands on the right by the railway lines. There are still fields visible to the north where houses were soon to be built.

Romford Railway Station and the Star Inn in 1856. Romford's first station building, a rather temporary affair stood on the embankment to the west of Dog Lane (now Waterloo Road) near the later cattle offloading dock and Romford West signal box.

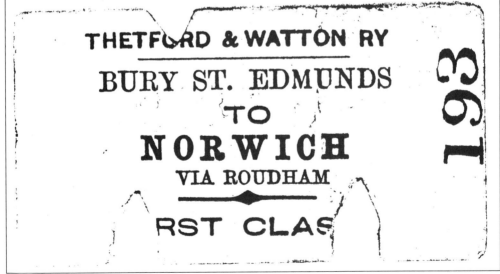

A ticket carrying the name of one of the many sections of the growing network. At the time each was defined as a separate railway but they were soon to be controlled by the larger entities such as the Eastern Counties. The efficient system of ticket inspection and control is evidenced by the fact that the card bears no less than three official clippings.

Two

Progress
by Land and Sea

A cattle box specially designed for attachment to passenger trains. The great number of smaller railways were brought together by the formation of the Great Eastern Railway created by an Act of Parliament in 1862.

Lea Bridge Station, opened in 1840. This imposing frontage built over the line displays the important status of railways in their early years. At the time of this photograph, around 1897, a half-hourly all-night service between Liverpool Street and Wood Street, Walthamstow had just been inaugurated to carry the many shift-workers in the City to and from their homes.

Lea Bridge Station from the trackside, 1897. For several years Lea Bridge was the railhead for the village of Walthamstow whose city gents were ferried to and fro by a local coach service. This was the situation between 1840 and 1870. A start had been made on embankments and cuttings for the Walthamstow and Chingford Branch in the 1860s but the financial and capital crisis of the new Great Eastern Railway led to a halt in the work.

Lea Bridge platform, 1907. The Great Eastern had formulated an ambitious plan to link new lines in North-East London with a new terminus at Liverpool Street, nearer the heart of the City of London. Many of the poorer working classes whose homes were destroyed in this construction were decanted out towards Walthamstow, into new housing estates.

G.E.R. passenger tank engine, No. 141 of 1864. Although the Great Eastern's plan had to be modified, once the financial crisis had been overcome the suburban network began to grow and the housing boom occurring demanded improved train services, many of which were worked by tank engines.

The Great Eastern Works at Stratford itself became a large employer and crowds of workers are here seen leaving one of the gates. The works were surrounded by a railway 'town' with railway estates such as 'Hudsons Town', named after the famous George Hudson, briefly Chairman of the Eastern Counties.

Plan of Stratford Works, 1862. It already had 32 separate divisions, plus an innovative Mechanics Institute with a gymnasium, library, school and baths. Later, during James Holden's 22 years as Loco, Carriage and Wagon Super-intendent(1885-1907), new 'Temple' workshop and a chemical laboratory were added.

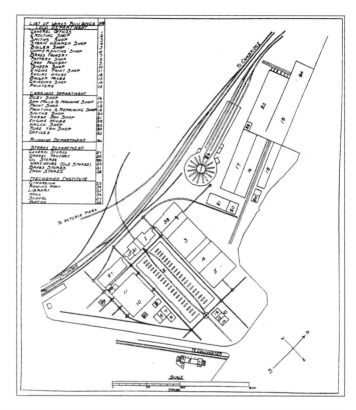

A 'Lowryesque' view of workers entering and leaving the largest railway works in England at Stratford about 1912. In a plan of this year no less than 61 buildings are identified in the complex of the main works, fitted in between a network of railway lines, with four entrance and exit gateways. 5,500 workers were employed.

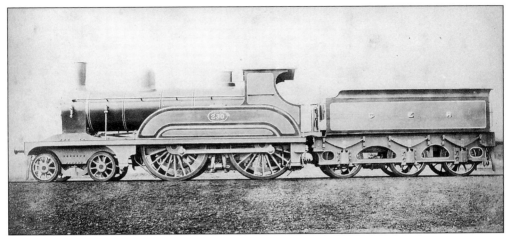

4-4-0 Locomotive No. 230. Eight G.E.R. loco Chiefs built and modified steam engines at Stratford between 1862 and 1922. They were R. Sinclair, S. W. Johnson, W. Adams, M. Bromley, T. W. Worsdell, J. Holden, S. D. Holden and A. J. Hill.

One of Adams 4-4-0 goods engines of 1877, No.266. Nicknamed 'Ironclads', they were scrapped in 1897.

0-6-0 Locomotive No.432.

Main Line Goods Engine No. 1189.

2-4-0 Locomotive No.1038, its tender piled high with coal.

Construction work at the Provender Works, Squirrels Heath. The preparation of horse-feed was transferred to this building from the old works next door – the sack and sheet factory remaining in the old building, an air view of which appears earlier in this book (see page 23).

Women workers print instructions on provender sacks at the Provender Works – the second
G.E.R. factory at Squirrels Heath in 1920. The Provender (hay and clover) processed here was
used to feed the horses (numbering 1,760 in 1912) owned by the Great Eastern.

A view of the machinery inside the provender stores, 1910.

The Provender Factory from the south around 1912. The main line between Romford and Essex runs on the far side. This building was dramatically burnt to the ground in 1968 when it had become a furniture factory/store.

A class at Factory Terrace, 1897. This was located in two cottages, rented from the railway company from 1858. Ephraim Loyd is fifth from the left, in the second row from the top. Mr London, the manager of the Romford Factory is dead centre in that row. In front of him is Mr Osman, the headmaster.

Ephraim Loyd aged 96 was still living in the Squirrels Heath area in the 1980s. Aged 12, he was called out of his class at school closing time and told he would be leaving to start work in the office at the old tarpaulin factory the next morning.

A. Kimber at work in the tarpaulin factory. For 40 he had made loin clothes and aprons for the railway horses out of odds and ends of cloths and discarded straps. He is seen here in January 1925.

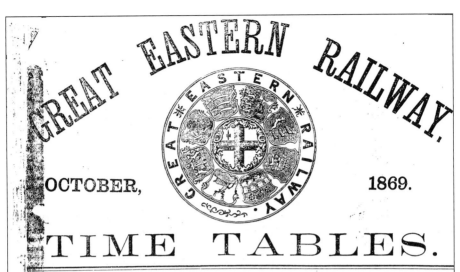

GREAT EASTERN RAILWAY.

OCTOBER, 1869.

TIME TABLES.

London and Blackwall, Woolwich, Woodford, Epping, Ongar, Enfield, Hertford, Buntingford, Saffron Walden, Cambridge, Newmarket, St Ives, Huntingdon, March, Peterborough, Wisbeach, Ely, Sutton, Lynn, Hunstanton, Burnham, Dereham, Fakenham, Wells, Norwich, Chelmsford, Maldon, Braintree, Sudbury, Haverhill, Bury St. Edmund's, Colchester, Brightlingsea, Walton-on-the-Naze, Hadleigh, Harwich, Ipswich, Bungay, Framlingham, Leiston, Aldborough, Lowestoft, Yarmouth, &c.

CONTINENTAL STEAM BOATS.

THE SHORTEST, CHEAPEST, AND MOST DIRECT ROUTE

VIA HARWICH,

TO

HOLLAND, GERMANY, THE RHINE,

BELGIUM, EAST OF FRANCE, AND SWITZERLAND.

THROUGH TICKETS TO THE CONTINENT

CAN BE OBTAINED AT THE FOLLOWING OFFICES:—

BISHOPSGATE TERMINUS. | BLOSSOMS INN, LAWRENCE LANE, CHEAPSIDE.

NO PASSPORTS REQUIRED by British subjects travelling via **HARWICH** to Holland, Germany, The Rhine, Belgium, and Switzerland.

BAGGAGE REGISTERED FROM BISHOPSGATE STATION.

NO SMALL BOATS USED.

FIRST CLASS HOTEL, *belonging to the Great Eastern Railway Company, now open at* **HARWICH,** *for Families, Tourists, &c.*

———— PRICE ONE PENNY. ————

Printed and Published by JOHN REA, of No. 1, Glamorgan Villas, Buxton Road, Stratford, in the County of Essex, at the Office of the Company, at Stratford, in the County of Essex, and Sold at all Stations on the Great Eastern Railway.

In their October 1869 timetable the Great Eastern, although still running from their cramped Bishopsgate, Shoreditch Terminus is heavily advertising their continental connections via Harwich.

Parkeston Station platforms and a glimpse of the hotel, 1912. Parkeston Quay, named after Charles H. Parkes, Chairman of the G.E.R. was built on causeway over marshy land as a substantial wooden structure in 1883. A wide northward loop of railway served it and went on to the original embarkation of Harwich Town.

The Great Eastern's steamer 'Brussels' at Antwerp' South Quay embarkation area, 1905.

GREAT EASTERN RAILWAY.

HOLLAND, GERMANY, THE RHINE,

BELGIUM, SWITZERLAND, AND ITALY,

VIA HARWICH.

IMPROVED TRAIN SERVICE FOR THE SUMMER.

PASSENGER SERVICE,

OCTOBER, 1869,

(Unless prevented by unforeseen circumstances).

LONDON TO ROTTERDAM.

Date.	From London.	From Harwich.	Due at Rotterdam about
Saturday, Oct. 2	8 30 p.m.	1 0 a.m.	1 0 p.m.
Tuesday, ,, 5	8 30 p.m.	4 0 a.m.	4 0 p.m.
Thursday, ,, 7	2 30 p.m.	5 0 p.m.	5 0 a.m.
Saturday, ,, 9	4 0 p.m.	6 30 p.m.	6 30 a.m.
Tuesday, ,, 12	7 0 p.m.	9 30 p.m.	9 30 a.m.
Thursday, ,, 14	8 30 p.m.	12 0 night	12 0 noon
Saturday, ,, 16	8 30 p.m.	1 30 a.m.	1 30 p.m.
Tuesday, ,, 19	8 30 p.m.	3 0 a.m.	3 0 p.m.
Thursday, ,, 21	8 30 p.m.	4 0 a.m.	4 0 p.m.
Saturday, ,, 23	3 0 p.m.	5 30 p.m.	5 30 a.m.
Tuesday, ,, 26	4 25 p.m.	7 30 p.m.	7 30 a.m.
Thursday, ,, 28	7 25 p.m.	10 0 p.m.	10 0 a.m.
Saturday, ,, 30	8 30 p.m.	12 15 night	12 15 noon

ROTTERDAM TO LONDON.

Date.	From Rotterdam.	From Harwich.	Due in London.
Saturday, Oct. 2	8 30 a.m.	9 0 p.m.	11 15 p.m.
Tuesday, ,, 5	10 30 a.m.	11 0 p.m.	1 15 a.m.
Thursday, ,, 7	12 0 noon	12 30 night	2 45 a.m.
Saturday, ,, 9	1 33 p.m.	2 0 a.m.	4 15 a.m.
Tuesday, ,, 12	4 0 p.m.	4 30 a.m.	6 45 a.m.
Thursday, ,, 14	6 30 a.m.	7 0 p.m.	9 15 p.m.
Saturday, ,, 16	8 30 a.m.	9 0 p.m.	11 15 p.m.
Tuesday, ,, 19	10 30 a.m.	11 0 p.m.	1 15 a.m.
Thursday, ,, 21	11 30 a.m.	12 0 night	2 15 a.m.
Saturday, ,, 23	12 0 noon	12 30 night	2 45 a.m.
Tuesday, ,, 26	2 0 p.m.	2 30 a.m.	4 45 a.m.
Thursday, ,, 28	3 30 a.m.	4 0 a.m.	6 15 a.m.
Saturday, ,, 30	6 30 a.m.	7 0 p.m.	9 15 p.m.

LONDON TO ANTWERP.

Every **WEDNESDAY** and **SATURDAY** at 4.25 p.m.; leaving Harwich at 8.0 p.m., arriving at Antwerp about 8.0 a.m.

ANTWERP TO LONDON.

Every **TUESDAY** and **FRIDAY** at 1.0 p.m.; leaving Harwich at 7.55 a.m., arriving in London at 10.40 a.m.

NOVEMBER, 1869.

LONDON TO ROTTERDAM.

Date.	From London.	From Harwich.	Due at Rotterdam about
Tuesday, Nov. 2	8 30 p.m.	2 0 a.m.	2 0 p.m.
Thursday, ,, 4	8 30 p.m.	3 30 a.m.	3 30 p.m.
Saturday, ,, 6	8 30 p.m.	5 0 a.m.	5 0 p.m.
Tuesday, ,, 9	4 0 p.m.	6 30 p.m.	6 30 a.m.
Thursday, ,, 11	6 30 p.m.	9 30 p.m.	10 0 a.m.
Saturday, ,, 13	8 15 p.m.	11 0 p.m.	11 0 a.m.
Tuesday, ,, 16	8 30 p.m.	2 0 a.m.	2 0 p.m.
Thursday, ,, 18	8 30 p.m.	3 0 a.m.	3 0 p.m.
Saturday, ,, 20	8 30 p.m.	4 0 a.m.	4 0 p.m.
Tuesday, ,, 23	3 30 p.m.	6 0 p.m.	6 0 a.m.
Thursday, ,, 25	4 25 p.m.	8 0 p.m.	8 0 a.m.
Saturday, ,, 27	6 30 p.m.	9 30 p.m.	10 0 a.m.
Tuesday, ,, 30	8 30 p.m.	1 0 a.m.	1 0 p.m.

ROTTERDAM TO LONDON.

Date.	From Rotterdam.	From Harwich.	Due in London.
Tuesday, Nov. 2	9 0 a.m.	12 45 night	4 30 a.m.
Thursday, ,, 4	11 0 a.m.	12 45 night	4 30 a.m.
Saturday, ,, 6	12 0 noon	12 45 night	4 30 a.m.
Tuesday, ,, 9	2 0 p.m.	3 0 a.m.	5 30 a.m.
Thursday, ,, 11	2 0 p.m.	3 0 a.m	5 30 a.m.
Saturday, ,, 13	6 30 a.m.	7 30 p.m.	9 45 p.m.
Tuesday, ,, 16	9 0 a.m.	12 45 night	4 30 a.m.
Thursday, ,, 18	10 30 a.m.	12 45 night	4 30 a.m.
Saturday, ,, 20	11 30 a.m.	12 45 night	4 30 a.m.
Tuesday, ,, 23	1 0 p.m.	2 0 a.m.	4 40 a.m.
Thursday, ,, 25	2 0 p.m	3 0 a.m	5 30 a.m.
Saturday, ,, 27	5 0 a.m.	5 30 p.m.	8 55 p.m.
Tuesday, ,, 30	8 30 a.m.	9 0 p.m.	11 15 p.m.

LONDON TO ANTWERP.

Every **WEDNESDAY** and **SATURDAY** at 4.25 p.m.; leaving Harwich at 8.0 p.m., arriving at Antwerp about 8.0 a.m.

ANTWERP TO LONDON.

Every **TUESDAY** and **FRIDAY** at 1.0 p.m.; leaving Harwich at 7.55 a.m., arriving in London at 10.40 a.m.

Return Tickets to Antwerp or Rotterdam are available on the Return Journey from either place.

Schedule of continental trains, October 1869. Note the headings 'due at Rotterdam about'. This uncertainty was caused by the steamers having to cross the Brielle bar, off the Dutch coast which could only be managed at high tide.

The quayside with cranes and steamer, *Parkeston*, c. 1914. Improvements to the continental services occurred all the time. The opening of the 'New Waterway' on the Dutch coast in March 1872 enabled the Brielle bar to be bypassed and Rotterdam steamers to run on fixed timetables.

The miniature, turbo-driven liner *S.S. Munich* at the Hook of Holand around 1911. On the night of 1 June 1893 the *S.S. Chelmsford* made the first sailing from Parkeston Quay to the Hook of Holland. This was a new port designed to save incoming steamers the time involved in the slow journey up the Maas to Rotterdam.

The G.E.R.'s Brussels steamship was taken over by the Admiralty in 1914. It was captured by the Germans on 22 June 1916. They charged the master Capt. Charles Fryatt with having attempted to ram the submarine which attacked his ship. He was shot at Bruges on 27 July 1916. This memorial gives the details.

This publicity for the G.E.R.'s continental trains and steamers appeared at the back of a 70-page
booklet 'New Holidays in Essex' edited by the well known agent Percy Lindley and published at
the end of the nineteenth century. This lyrically described the G.E.R.'s Essex extension lines as
they are referred to. On the facing page a short description is given of various continental tours
with specimen fares and such helpful comments as "Living in the Luxemburg Ardennes ranges
from 4–5 shillings a day".

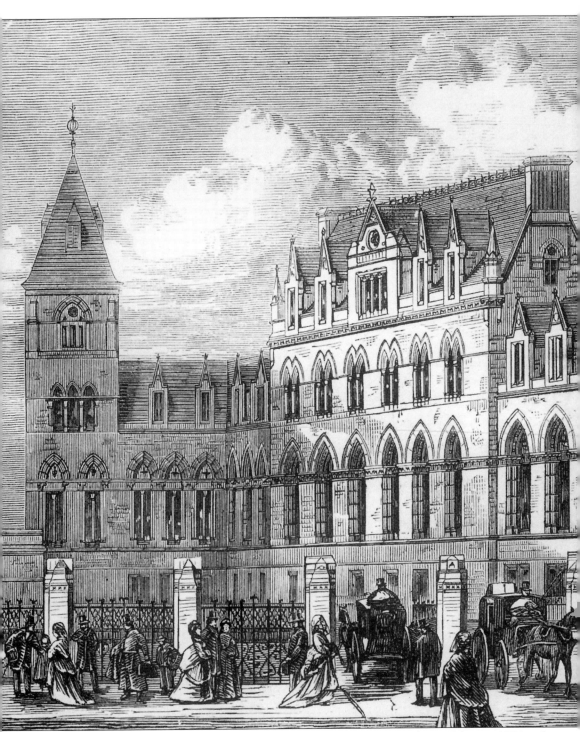

The new Liverpool Street Terminus, the first part of which was opened on 2 February 1874 and the rest on 1 November 1875, ten years after approval had been given by Act of Parliament. The scheme involved a new line of railway passing below and to one side of the former Bishopsgate Terminus and swooping round to the new station. The General Manager at the

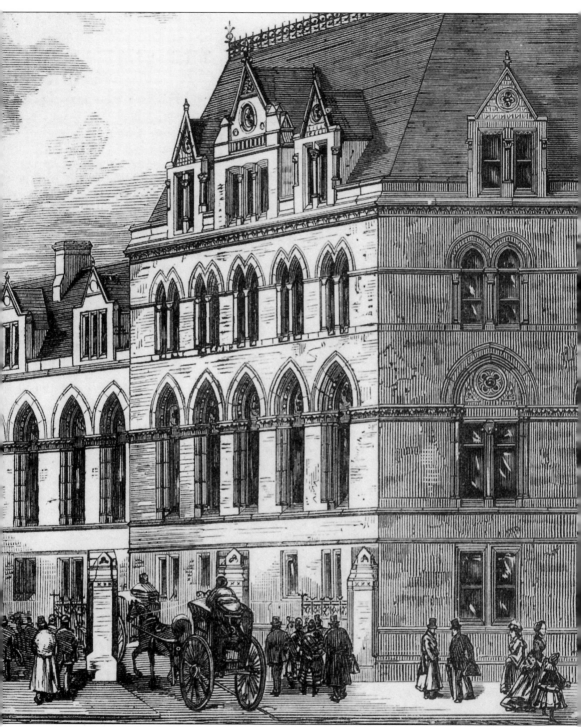

time, Samual Swarbrick, was the guiding genius behind the scheme and would not let any director deter him, not even the formidable Salisbury, later to be Prime Minister nor Lord Hamilton who both had reservations about the expense.

Six-wheeled passenger coach with first and second class compartments and luggage space. Second class disappeared from most trains on the G.E.R. on 1 January 1893. It remained only on London suburban services and continental expresses. The two classes from then on during

much of the twentieth century were first and third – only in fairly recent years was third converted into second class.

Kitson tank engine, 0-4-4.

The Southwold Railway was a quaint independent line which lasted from 1879-1929, serving the small communities in the midst of Great Eastern territory.

Impression of the delightful G.E.R. restaurant car – an illustration from the booklet 'Seaside and Countryside in East Anglia' published around 1920. The G.E.R.'s first restaurant car facility was on its North Country Continental Express (Harwich–York) from 1 July 1891. By the summer of 1913, eleven restaurant cars trains left Liverpool Street between 4.55 p.m. (Cromer) and 12 midnight (Southend supper train) – no other London terminus could equal this succession.

Liverpool Street scene about 1895 – a Tilling bus (Liverpool Street to Peckham and Dulwich Park route) passes the familiar gatepost. Behind looms the bulk of the North London Railway's Broad Street Terminus, opened in 1865 and designed by William Baker. At the turn of the

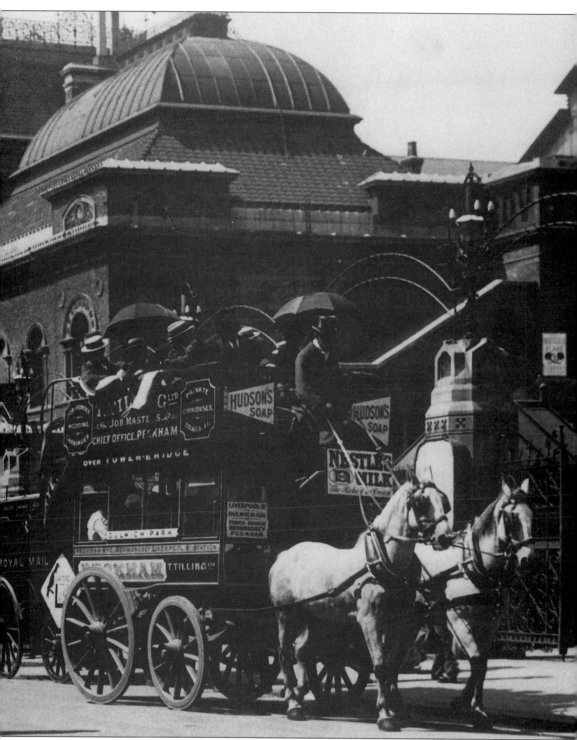

century this had become London's third busiest station – Liverpool Street being first. Quite soon however Broad Street declined – the bus, the tram and the underground railway took away most of its passengers – a threat to which the Great Eastern's suburban routes were not immune.

A train manoeuvres into Wickford Station, 1907. The Shenfield–Wickford extension, one of the new Essex lines, opened on 19 November 1888.

Three
Expansion to Suburbia

Railway at the end of the Coborn Road, Bow around 1912. At this time Bow still felt almost like a suburb with its railed front gardens, and its convenient station, ensuring a fast ride into the City. This convenience was lost from 1 May 1916 when wartime savings forced the G.E.R. to announce the 'Closure of Stations' – namely Barkingsidem Bethnal Green, Bradfield, Buckenham, Cambridge Heath, Chigwell Lane, Coborn Road, Earsham, Geldeston, Globe Road, Leman Street, London Fields, Mardock, Shadwell, Stanhoe and West Mill. These were either rural stations or in the city at a short distance from each other. Although reopened eventually, Coborn Road had lost its passing trade to the increasingly popular trams and motor buses.

Railway Station   ~~Many Happy returns of~~   *Forest Gate*

Published by W. G. Barton, 82 Upton Lane, Forest Gate

Busy Forest Gate Station entrance, 1903. The suburbs had moved outward in the Edwardian years. In 1844 traffic had grown so sparse at this fledgling station that it was actually closed for a while.

Trams on the prowl for local passengers outside Forest Gate Station, 1908.

52

1906 platform scene at Forest Gate – train about to leave. In 1901 there were 450 daily trains in winter and 520 passing through in summer. There had been a special suburban service ending at this point for several years. This service was now being extended to Ilford as the suburbs spread outwards and additional tracks were laid to the latter station.

1910 saw the building of a new station at Squirrels Heath and Gidea Park just beyond Romford – this unusual photograph shows the earliest stage of platform construction.

The completed Squirrels Heath and Gidea Park with its signal box curiously suspended on girders above the platform. Avenues of trees still abound in the fields around.

A 1500 class 4-6-0 engine heads a train of mixed stock at Gidea Park and Squirrel's Heath – the stations name was inverted after a few years, The Great Eastern's intention was to acquire commuters from the newly built Gidea Park Garden Suburb, a superior development to the east of Romford. A publicity campaign was launched and a large number of attractive booklets extolling the virtues of the estate and the conveniently adjacent Great Eastern station were produced by the G.E.R. and developers working in conjunction. There were special concessionary fares for travellers visiting the new suburb. Today a commuter service from London still terminates at Gidea Park.

Forty Hill Station from Turkey Street. One of three stations on a new line opened in October 1891 to cater for development north-east of Edmonton. The development did not happen and the line closed, 1 October 1909. Amazingly it was reopened in the 1950s to form part of a new electrified route to Broxbourne, Hertford and Bishop Stortford.

Seven Kings Station entrance, 1907. The Ilford District, on the East Anglia main line was the scene of incredible development in late Victorian and Edwardian times. There were amazing increases in commuter traffic resulting in the opening of this station.

In between two sets of lines at Loughton Station, 1910. The sidings and the main route to Ongar gives the appearance of a junction between two lines. This line to Epping and Ongar attracted the Epping Forest tourist traffic but also served farms and other rural enterprises.

Snaresbrook's steep approach, 1906. The station also served Wanstead.

Snaresbrook and Wanstead Station platform level scene. The construction of the Woodford and Ilford line, which opened in May 1905, completed a loop enabling a circular service to be run through this point.

Noel Park and Wood Green on the Palace Gates Branch, seen in 1904 was a north-west London outpost encroaching on Great Northern territory.

Waltham Cross Station G. E. R.

Waltham Cross with its churns, horse traps and early motor-vehicle collecting an important traveller summarises the traffic situation in 1906, on Cheshunt and Cambridge main line.

Bruce Grove Station, Tottenham in a fairly well-built-up suburb, 1905 on the Silver Street line which joined up with the main Cambridge line at Cheshunt. We see again the G.E.R.'s penchant for publicising their routes into London on all the available station bridges. A board beside the entrance claims that the G.E.R. is the quickest route to various London destinations, adding the inducement 'Low Fares'. Such publicity must have made quite an impact on the numbers of people who passed daily.

Four
Rails through Essex

Colchester's old wooden station building around 1904. This point was as far as the original Eastern Counties reached in its initial thrust towards Norwich. The Eastern Union railway took up the baton and surveyed and built their line to Ipswich. Their plan was to build a Colchester Station of their own a few hundred yards north of the Eastern Counties and join up with the Eastern Counties half-a-mile further towards London. This would have avoided the curve of the Eastern Counties line which had tried to approach as near as possible to the foot of Colchester hill. However it was agreed that the companies should share the E.C.R. station and the curve into it severely slowed main line traffic throughout the Great Eastern days.

Brentwood Station, c. 1905, showing the old station buildings in use on the up platform. On the right is another of the G.E.R.'s platform signalboxes.

A view over the down platform, Brentwood from the bridge in 1908. A train is approaching the up side. Note the small turret on the roof from which it is said a bell announced the trains. On the left, in the station yard, there is a cab rank and cabmen's shelter.

A down train pulls in to Brentwood on a dull day around 1910. The building on the right is the
Brentwood engine shed which has recently had a new roof fitted.

The Seven Arch Bridge, Brentwood 1906, a favourite area for taking photographs of the G.E.R. trains over the decades. Brentwood Bank towards Shenfield was the first severe test of loco power in Essex and a serious accident took place here in the earliest days of the Eastern Counties Railway.

Chelmsford Station frontage around 1908 with various horse-drawn vehicles awaiting trains. A viaduct carries the East Anglian main line over the town.

A line of porters and other railwaymen watch the cameraman at work on the up platform, where a crowd of passengers and luggage expectantly awaits the arrival of a London train, 1913.

G.E.R. motor bus waiting outside Clacton Station, 1905. The Tendring Hundred Railway reached Clacton in July 1882. In 1901 a start was made on assembling the first G.E.R. buses at Stratford works. In 1902 the buses went on road trial, visiting places such as Clacton and St Osyth.

Dunmow Station on the Braintree–Bishops Stortford line was opened in February 1869 as a single track railway. The great importance of goods traffic is evidenced by the tarpaulined goods wagons, c. 1907.

Witham Station on the Colchester main line with a London Train on the centre tracks and goods wagons lurking on the far lines, 1911. This was the junction for the Maldon–Witham–Braintree line, opened in 1848. Braintree was then connected with Bishops Stortford in 1869 and Maldon also connected with Wickford on the Southend Line, making Witham a crossroads on the G.E.R. system.

From J. Belsham & Son.

Please forward the heap
of firewood No. 23 now at
Hatfield Peverel to Rayne
Station — our order.

Braintree.
3 August 1915.

Typical of thousands of small goods transactions is this card posted on the 4th August 1915 to E.L. Hawkins, District Engineer, Ipswich asking for firewood at Hatfield Peverel to be transported to Rayne Station.

Hockley Station with its partially staggered platforms in 1907. Wicker baskets of goods have been wheeled out for carriage by the incoming train.

Rayleigh Station around 1916 – a rustic touch is provided by the ornamental bush next to the signalbox. The new Southend Line was completed from Wickford to Southend and opened on 1st October 1889.

Level crossing at South Woodham on the Southminster line, which diverged from Wickford, opening on 1st June 1889. The whole line was a rural backwater during Great Eastern days.

In 1905 Shenfield's importance lay in the fact that it was the junction of the East Anglian main line and the Southend branch with it connections to Southminster and Maldon. Its significant growth as a commuter station was to occur only after the Great Eastern had been absorbed into the L.N.E.R.

No. 393   The Old L & N E Rly. Station, Shenfield

The clear view of the track and trains visible from outside the old station at Shenfield. Some signs of the coming expansion are seen in the three motor taxis outside in the early 1920s. The station, running lines, platforms and bridge were all to be considerably enlarged.

Tiptree Station and sidings about 1915, looking like a railway scene in the wilds of Australia or America.

Wivenhoe's sharply curving platform seen in 1913. The railway from Hythe to Wivenhoe opened on 8th May 1863.

Unloading at Hockley – a mini rush hour. Note the familiar standard footbridge pattern.

Panoramic view of Marks Tey, 1898. Three trains are visible, one on the main line to the left, with passenger and goods trains on the Stour Valley Railway metals to the right. The S.V.R. was opened in july 1849 as an independent line between Colchester and Sudbury – a previous branch between Colchester and Hythe having begun operation on 31st March 1847.

Five
To Poppyland and Back

Ipswich station interchange point with the local tramway system. The original Eastern Union Station on a site adjacent to the River Orwell at Griffins Wharf, south of Stoke Hill, avoided the necessity of tunnelling through the hill. However very shortly another company, the Ipswich and Bury Railway, built a line to Bury St. Edmunds and grasped the nettle – tunnelling through Stoke Hill. The new main line station at Ipswich was built north of the tunnel and the two companies, having many directors in common decided to share the more convenient station.

Goods wagons on an old track by the Custom House at Ipswich. The Ipswich and Bury started to work as one with the Eastern Union, no more than a week after the opening of the former on 7th December 1846.

The Yarmouth Express at Brentwood's Seven Arch Bridge, 1904. These special trains were the G.E.R.'s pride and joy, especially their elegant restaurant car facilities.

Needham Market's extraordinary station architecture in 1916 – one of three fine stations built on the Ipswich and Bury line in the Elizabethan style, the others being Stowmarket and Bury St. Edmunds.

Railway Station,
Newmarket.

A study of the platform awning contrasted with a typical G.E.R. platform scene with bookstall
and train at Newmarket, 1912.

Norwich Thorpe Station's commanding situation as terminus of the original Norfolk Railway
compared favourably with the out-of-the-way Victoria Station into which the Eastern Union
Norwich extension trains ran.

The double-headed Cromer express, 1904. G.E.R. publicists such as Percy Lindley helped to create the idea of Poppyland – a glamorous name for North Norfolk's coastline.

Cromer Lighthouse, 1906, one of the symbols of Poppyland. A drawing or photograph of a local feature like this would be used many times in publicity for the G.E.R.'s Norfolk resorts.

Sheringham Sands, 1908 – presented in the Great Eastern's literature as a new resort served well by the G.E.R.'s summer expresses.

The Great Eastern's Hotel at Hunstanton. A view from the booklet 'On the East Coast' published in 1911, by Percy Lindley the G.E.R.'s publicist.

SANDRINGHAM HOTEL, HUNSTANTON

Hunstanton's Sandringham Hotel. The Company's hotels were part of the overall plan to lure tourists to Norfolk via the train – hardly anyone possessed a motorcar for holiday journeys in 1920.

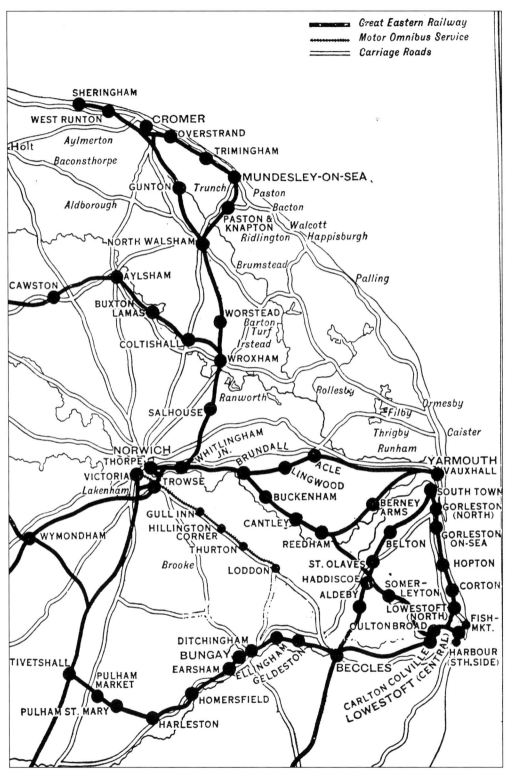

Map of lines to the Norfolk coast from the booklet 'On the East Coast', 1911.

Six

Promoting the Line

The Great Eastern's restaurant car service had a high reputation for the quality of food, service and comfort. It was an effective way of promoting travel by Great Eastern expresses to the coast.

GREAT EASTERN RAILWAY.

CHEAP TRIP TO
LONDON AND BACK THE SAME DAY.

ON THURSDAY, 15th September,
A SPECIAL EXCURSION TRAIN
WILL RUN AS UNDER :—

From	Train at	Fares to London and Back.	
		First Class.	Covered Cars.
	Morn.		
MALDON ...	6 30		
WITHAM	6 50	5s. 0d.	2s. 6d.
CHELMSFORD	7 15		
LONDON, arr. about	8 30		

Returning from London at 8 p.m. the same day.

The Tickets may be obtained at the Stations from Tuesday, 13th September, and will be available only by the Special Train as above.
No Luggage allowed, except a Small Bag or Parcel carried by the Owner.

By order,

J. B. OWEN, Secretary.

London, *August 11th.* 1864.

Early advertising in local newspapers spread the news about the company's excursion trains, 1864. Stations and booking-offices were sometimes overwhelmed by the number of potential excursionists turning up on the day.

Seaside and Countryside by the Great Eastern Railway

Edited by Percy Lindley

The title page of a 1920 booklet promoting the Summer Train Service to the coast. The 64 pages contained over 50 charming illustrations, including 28 in colour with descriptions of the coastal and inland scenery.

The Staithe, Horsey Mere – one of the G.E.R.'s postcards which could be bought in sets (2 old pence for 5 cards in 1914).

Cranbrook Castle, Ilford on a G.E.R. postcard, reminds us that many parts of Greater London were suitable for country walks, before and after the First World War.

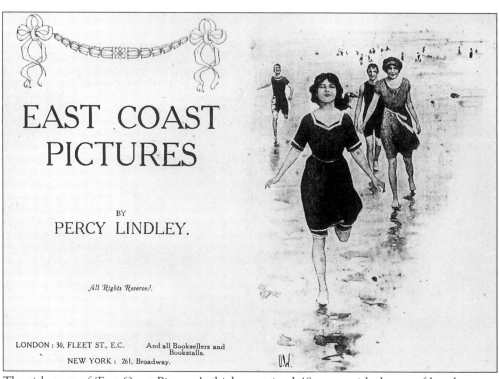

EAST COAST PICTURES

BY

PERCY LINDLEY.

LONDON : 30, FLEET ST., E.C.   And all Booksellers and
Bookstalls.
NEW YORK : 261, Broadway.

The title page of 'East Coast Pictures' which contained 48 pages with dozens of beach scenes illustrated from Hunstanton down to Southend and details of G.E.R. trains, tickets, continental boats and hotels summarised in the final pages.

On the

East Coast

By PERCY LINDLEY.

For List of Golf Links see pages 64-67.

LONDON : 30, Fleet Street, E.C.   And all Booksellers and Bookstalls
NEW YORK : 261, Broadway.

Summer Seaside Services.

THE facilities for reaching the East Coast at all seasons, both as regards train service and cheap fares may be said to be unique. The coast line is linked with London by a fine express service of corridor and restaurant trains, morning, afternoon and evening.

Luxurious trains in addition to affording every modern convenience for passengers' comfort, provide the shortest, quickest, and most convenient service between Liverpool Street Station—which is accessible from all parts of London—and the East Coast.

The services are so arranged that visitors can travel daily to and fro, taking luncheon, tea, dinner or supper on the journey down, and breakfast and other meals on the journey up.

Numerous improvements in the services figure in the summer programme, although continual additions and accelerations during recent seasons leave little scope for any marked changes. Last season, for instance, upwards of 45 trains a day ran between London and the twenty seaside resorts served by the Great Eastern Railway Company.

The full summer service commences this year on July 1st.

Page from 'East Coast Pictures' published just before the First World War extolling the delights of the company's 'luxury trains' Tourist information about the Cromer Coast and the Broads covered several pages each. Individual resorts such as Aldeburgh, Southwold and Felixstowe rated a page of text and a fullpage illustration opposite, in sepia.

Opposite, left: Postcard of the Ancient House at Ipswich in the G.E.R. series. Right: Title page of 'On the East Coast' published 1911 with Art-Nouveau style cover.

ON THE EAST COAST.

For the least rain and the most sunshine, holiday-makers must go, according to the recording Weather Clerk, to the breezy East Coast.

On this authority while the rainfall last year at Clacton, for instance, was only 21 inches, at Brighton it was over 32 inches. And while Felixstowe, as another instance, had 1,768 hours of sunshine, Brighton had only 1,690 hours.

These favoured weather conditions, shared by other East Coast resorts, are not so well known, perhaps, as they should be. For dry days and sunny days lengthen our holidays, especially for the growing crowd of golfers and week-enders, all the year round, and for the greater crowd of those who take summer day trips and half-day trips whenever they can.

And the sunshine is being brought nearer every season to London, and the North and Midlands. This summer the Great Eastern Railway is linking up the East Coast with a finer holiday service than ever, week-day and Sunday.

It provides express trains, non-stop trains, Restaurant trains, morning, afternoon and evening. This train acceleration benefits the East Coast from the Thames to the Wash ; from Southend and Clacton, for the convenience of residents and business men travelling daily, as well as holiday-makers, right round the Essex, Suffolk, and Norfolk Coast.

In a word, the Great Eastern Company's programme should be studied by all who want the longest time and the best time by the sea with the greatest number of fine days, the sunshine, and the breeze. East Anglia to-day may be said to be an actual lung of London.

SOUTHEND.

Introduction to 'On the East Coast'

From Theydon Bois to Epping.

(See Map No. 4.)

DISTANCES.

From Theydon Bois to Ambresbury Banks .. $1\frac{1}{2}$ *miles.*

„ „ „ *Epping Station* .. $3\frac{1}{2}$ „

TURNING westward from the Railway Station at Theydon Bois (always pronounced Boys) through the avenue, we soon come to St. Mary's Church. The old Church stood

Page from 'Epping Forest' by F.H.Headley, a pioneering Great Eastern booklet of 63 pages printed at the G.E.R.'s works at Stratford. As well as a description of four walks in the Forest it contained fascinating facts about the history and natural history, with five ingenious fold-out maps at the end. The booklet has continued to appear in revised editions under the G.E.R.'s successors.

HERE'S HEALTH
TO EVERYBODY!

THE
GREAT EASTERN Rℓʸ Cº

OFFERS A CHOICE
OF OVER TWENTY
OF ENGLAND'S MOST
POPULAR HOLIDAY
RESORTS, ON A
BEAUTIFUL COAST
AMIDST CHARMING
SURROUNDINGS···

An illustrated booklet "On the East Coast" with programme of cheap travel facilities & train arrangements will be sent gratis on application to Publicity Dept. Nº2, Superintendents' Office Liverpool Sᵗ, Station. E.C.

Here's Health to Everybody. This nautical figure graced the pages of various magazines around 1912. There is a slight 'hype' involved in calling East Anglia's resorts 'Twenty of England's most popular holiday resorts' (apart from Southend of course).

Seven

Danger Ahead
Tales of Pitch-ins

These huge gantries of semaphore signals were once a common feature of busy railway junctions as here at Stratford. The Great Eastern experimented with and used a number of systems, including Saxby's. An experimental electro-pneumatic installation was tried out at Spitalfields Goods Yard in 1899 (Mckenzie, Holland and Westinghouse system) but all-electric signalling did not come in until after G.E.R. days. The complex nature of signalling in parts of the G.E.R. was explained by the fact that the company was not known to have built a single burrowing or flying junction during its reign.

Hand Signals.

Hand signals. 27. These signals will be made by hand, or with flags by day ; and with lamps by night, or in foggy weather.

Danger signal. 28. **In the absence of Flags—** Both arms raised above the head denotes "Danger," thus :—

Caution signal. One arm raised above the head denotes "Caution," thus :—

All Right signal. One arm held in a horizontal position across the line of rails denotes "All Right," thus :—

Any light waved violently denotes "Danger." 29. In the absence of a red light, any light waved violently, denotes "Danger."—Stop.

NOTE.—*On the Eastern and Midlands, Great Northern, Hull and Barnsley, and London Brighton*

These hand signals appeared in the Rules and Regulations of the Great Eastern as late as 1889 and are reminiscent of those used by the early railway police.

A large number of Great Eastern signalboxes were located on platforms as here at Woodham Ferrers around 1907.

A Short Account of the work done by the Engineering Department during the last fifty years.

By J. H. WARDLEY, A.M. Inst.C.E.

FIFTY years ago great activity was being displayed in experimenting with different forms of rails and permanent way fastenings. Many of the conditions which it is necessary for them to fulfil were under-

Several types were flat based or vignole iron rails weighing from 40 to 72 lb. per yard of length and were attached by iron " dog " spikes to wooden sleepers laid transversely to the line. The rolls at

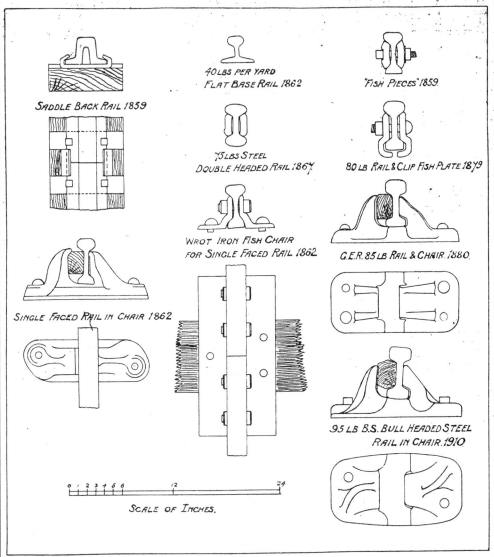

SADDLE BACK RAIL 1859

40 LBS PER YARD
FLAT BASE RAIL 1862

"FISH PIECES" 1859.

75 LBS STEEL
DOUBLE HEADED RAIL 1867.

80 LB RAIL & CLIP FISH PLATE 1879

WROT IRON FISH CHAIR
FOR SINGLE FACED RAIL 1862.

G.E.R. 85 LB RAIL & CHAIR 1880.

SINGLE FACED RAIL IN CHAIR 1862.

95 LB B.S. BULL HEADED STEEL
RAIL IN CHAIR 1910.

0 1 2 3 4 5 6   12   24
SCALE OF INCHES.

TYPES OF RAILS AND CHAIRS USED AT DIFFERENT DATES.

stood so imperfectly that in 1862, when the 17 Companies amalgamated to form the Great Eastern system, the types of rails were very numerous.

the iron mills were so arranged that the web and head of the rail were not perpendicular to the base ; this caused the heads of the two rails of a track to

A factor in rail safety has been the development of rails and chairs used for the track. This illustration of evolving types was published to commemorate 50 years of the G.E.R. in 1912.

The horrifying scene on Witham Station platform after the wreck of the Cromer Express on 1st September 1905.

Wreckage is strewn across the track and platform at Witham in September 1905 – These pictures are by a local photographer Fred Spalding.

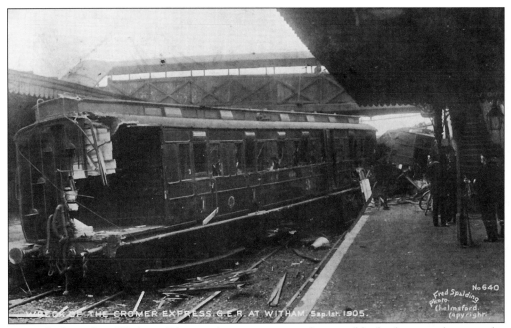

A wrecked coach at Witham. The accident was apparently caused by broken couplings on the fourth coach as it passed under the footbridge.

The coach plunged across the line towards the up platform causing the fifth coach to turn over. Ten people were killed, including a member of the staff who had been on the platform.

Signals at Wickford Station controlling the main-line and run-round bays, 1908.

A sad end to the Norfolk Coast Express-the Colchester accident, 12th July 1913.

Cromer Express Disaster. 12.7.13.

Pub.by Cullingford&Co. 1

The Colchester accident, showing the crushed coach behind the engine. The express had crashed into a light engine while travelling at full speed.

Overleaf: The story of the wreck of the Cromer–London Express summarised on a postcard. This was produced not by a local publisher but by W.Gothard of Barnsley who had made it his business to follow up disasters around the country including mine disasters and railway accidents.

TO LONDON EXPRESS

While the train was travelling at full speed it crashed into a light Engine, near to Colchester Station. The Driver and Fireman in charge of it were killed outright, the Guard died while being conveyed to the Hospital. The Driver of the light Engine, noticing the approach of the Express, put on full steam and tried desperately to get away, but having only a few seconds in which to act, was unable to avert the terrible disaster.

The smashed coaches and engine on its side at Colchester pictured by the local firm of Whitfield Cosser & Co.

The rescuers in conference at the scene of the Colchester smash. Photograph by F.Morter & Co., Military Road, Colchester.

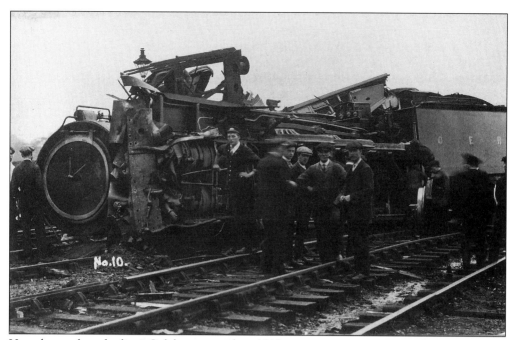

How do we clear the line? Colchester accident 1913.

At work clearing the wreckage, Colchester 1913.

<u>Copy</u>

60 Wellwood Road,

Goodmayes
2nd. Jan. 1915

Dear Sir,

I beg to give formal notice that
I was a passenger in the 8.34 a.m.
train - Goodmayes to Liverpool St.-
which came into collision with the
Clacton Express at Ilford yesterday.
I am under the care of my doctor,
and in due course intend to issue a
claim against your Company.

Yours faithfully

(Signed) J.H.Thomas
(2nd. class Season Ticket Holder)
No. 7 1.

The General Manager,

Great Eastern Rly. Co.,

Liverpool Street Station,

London, E.C.

After the Ilford accident of New Year's Day 1915, a victim writes to the G.E.R. to let them
know he will be making a damages claim.

Cranes at work after the Ilford accident.

The scene on the embankment after the Ilford accident.

```
                         Great Eastern Railway

                         Office of Superintendent of the Line,

                              Liverpool Street Station,

   C.7/16369/              London, E.C. February 16th, 1915.

Dear Sirs,

                re "Mr John Hugh Thomas".

     I beg to acknowledge receipt of your letter of the 15th

instant, and am having a cheque for £44-2-0 drawn as desired.   In

the meantime, will you kindly obtain your Client's signature to

the attached form of agreement, when I shall be pleased to hand

over the cheque in exchange for the document, and a receipt for

the money.

                    Yours faithfully,

                         pro Wm. C. May

                              Chief Traffic Manager.


Messrs.Sanderson Adkin Lee & Eddis,
          Solicitors,
               46, Queen Victoria Street,
                    E.C,
```

The Great Eastern pays compensation as described in this letter to the Solicitors of an Ilford accident victim.

Eight
Great Eastern People

Four white-collar staff at Stratford Works – photographed by E. Catherall, 44 Great Eastern Road, Stratford.

Station staff at Histon, Cambridgeshire in the early years of the century.

A line-up of coachbuilders at Stratford Works in 1920.

Servants of the Great Eastern, 1900 – the location is not known.

Ladies at work in the polishing shop. The First World War had brought women workers to the fore.

Ladies of the General Office, Liverpool Street, 1917. Barrels and goods train in the background.

Further lady members of the General Office staff, Liverpool Street, with a passenger train in background, 1917.

Cover of a later Great Eastern Railway Magazine. First produced in 1911, this set a very high standard and continued until the end of 1926.

Dining car crew on the G.E.R.'s York–Harwich service in the early 1900s. This was the first G.E.R. restaurant car running July 1891 onwards.

Young Great Eastern Railway porter on his way to work.

Long service Guard poses in his G.E.R. uniform at home.

GREAT
EASTERN
RAILWAY.

Chairman: S. A. PARNWELL, Esq.

𝔓rogramme

— OF —

FIRST ANNUAL

SMOKING CONCERT

OF THE

Staff of the Secretary and Comptroller,

HELD IN THE

Cambridge Room, Liverpool Street Hotel,

ON

Friday, 28th March, 1919, 7 p.m.

Mr. G. W. H. Cox

Programme for the First Annual Smoking Concert of the Secretary and Controllers Department in the Cambridge Room, Liverpool Street Hotel, issued to G.W.H. Cox. With the end of the war, the organisers obviously believe in a peaceful future stretching ahead.

A relaxed photograph of G.E.R. Station staff and family in the Newmarket area.

Nine
The Magic of a Railway

Front view of James Holden's 'Decapod', a wonderful piece of engineering which proved to the sceptics that an acceleration equal to that obtained with electricity could also be attained with steam traction. This was at a time when electrification of railways was very much on the agenda in Britain. 'Decapod was completed at the end of 1902. A test area was set up near Chadwell Heath to give an electrical recording of the rate of acceleration. The test took place from February–June 1903 when the engine was run between Stratford and Brentwood. After various adjustments Holden had the satisfaction of seeing his machine move a load of 18 four-wheeled coaches, specially weighted with pig iron to a total weight of 335 tons from a standing start up to the prescribed 30 m.p.h. in just under the specified 30 seconds.

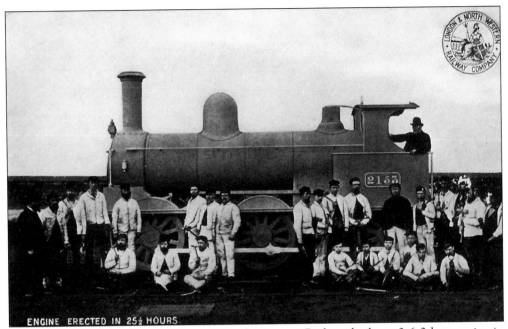

This proud team from the London and North Western Railway built an 0-6-0 locomotive in 1888 in 25½ working hours at Crewe.

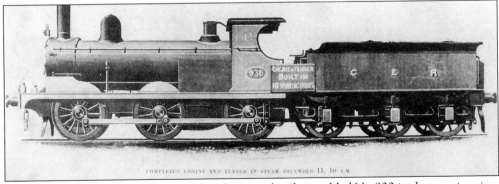

Stratford Works staff, determined to beat this record and assembled No.930 in the amazing time of 9 hours 47 minutes – a few hours later it began intensive duty on coal trains.

The G.E.R. Chelmsford – Danbury bus at the Griffin Hotel, Danbury in 1906. Other services ran from Chelmsford to Great Waltham and Writtle.

Parade of Great Eastern bus staff in front of a Great Waltham bus about 1906. Lowestoft, Oulton and Southwold were also served by 16 daily trips.

Liverpool Street, 1907 – a busy scene outside the entrance ramp to the West Side.

Staircase down to West Side platforms, Liverpool Street, 1909. At the back are the two long platforms that divided the station into two halves.

Looking across platforms 9 and 10 at Liverpool Street – the long platform roads for main line arrivals and departures – a footbridge above connected the West to the East Side of the station.

A view underneath the famous four-sided clock towards the west side. Note the elegant lamp, 1905.

A 'Claud Hamilton' Class 4-4-0 Express Passenger engine No.1831. This most well known G.E.R. loco class was both efficient and glamorous.

Side view of the ten-coupled tank Decapod – the most powerful engine in the world – the first 0-10-0 in Britain.

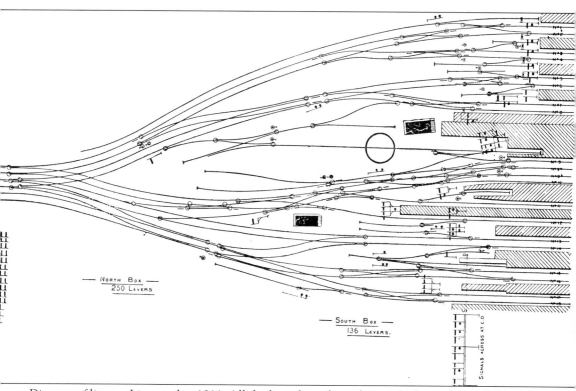

Diagram of lines at Liverpool in 1911. All the lines from the eighteen platforms channelled into 3 pairs of running lines out of the station.

New Suburban services display board. A new plan of ingenious alterations put into operation in 1920 enabled a highly intensive passenger service to be worked into and out of Liverpool Street without resorting to electrification.

The Great Eastern's second terminus – Fenchurch Street, 1909. This came to the Great Eastern in 1866 when the Blackwall Railway was leased to the G.E.R. for 999 years. The London

Tilbury and Southend Railway also shared the station. An interesting combination of destinations is shown on the departure board as awnings protect the roof which is under repair.

The neatly arranged and well-equipped kitchen-car of the Norfolk Coast Express. Restaurant Cars were one of the G.E.R.'s major successes – they appeared on Liverpool Street to Cromer and Yarmouth express trains in May 1899. The catering on these services was highly praised by international and British travellers of distinction.

Ten

From the Guard's Van – A Last Look

A rush of travellers at Liverpool Street in 1920. These crowds and more were what the 1920 improvements known as 'The Last Word in Steam Operated Suburban Train Services' were meant to manage. The G.E.R.'s proud boast was that it achieved a $2\frac{1}{2}$ minute service over the same line of rails using steam engines as small as the Holden 0-6-0 tanks. No other railway achieved this feat before or since with any kind of steam operation.

During the 1911 rail strike, soldiers are seen here beside the track guarding the railway at Temple Mill.

Soldiers bivouacing on Hackney Marshes in Great Eastern territory during the rail strike of 1911.

A result of the rather chaotic era of competition – the two competing stations at Romford. The Great Eastern main line on the left and the 'Tilbury' (taken over by the Midland Railway) station for the branch line to Upminster on the right.

The spacious forecourt of Braintree station, 1912 – goods traffic was an important factor on these mid-Essex railway links.

Inside the main entrance of the Liverpool Street Hotel 1907, The lobby is very up-to-date for the period with cane chairs and neat electroliers.

The lounge in the Abercorn Rooms, Liverpool Street Hotel – a smart place to hold meetings.

The waiting and refreshment room at Parkeston Quay, Harwich. H.C. Amendt, who controlled the Great Eastern's refreshment rooms and hotels, was a genius who set a high standard.

THE COMPANY'S HOTELS.

LIVERPOOL STREET.—In London the Company have a comfortable up-to-date hotel, central for business or pleasure, adjoining the station. Passengers walk direct from hotel to platform.

FELIXSTOWE.—The Felix Hotel stands high on the cliffs, with terraced gardens sloping to the beach, and enjoys seawards a full southern aspect. With its delightful palm court, noble reception-rooms, and open colonnades, overlooking beautiful lawns and flower gardens, the Felix, with its two hundred and fifty rooms, ranks as the finest hotel in East Anglia. Grass and hard tennis courts adjoin the hotel and the golf links are close at hand.

FELIX HOTEL, FELIXSTOWE

60

The Felix Hotel had just been acquired in 1920 when it was featured in the publicity booklet 'Seaside and Countryside'.

Seawater is loaded into a delivery vehicle at Liverpool Street having been brought by train from Lowestoft. Seawater Baths were provided in the Liverpool Street Hotel and barrels were offered for sale. In a July 1914 timetable an advert mentions that it 'is delivered Daily from Lowestoft to any part of London, including G.E. Suburban Stations, within the Company's Ordinary Cartage Delivery radius 6 old pence per 3 gallon'. Another service advertised was the conveyance of 'Small Parcels of Fish, 4d for 16 lbs, 6d for 24 lbs, are conveyed direct from fish merchants ... to Private Families in London.'